Production

and

Purchasing Management

:: Author ::

Nilamben H. Sondarva

(M.COM.,B.ed., SLET)

PUBLISHED BY

Hemchandracharya International Publishing House
HQ. At & Po. Chaveli., Ta- Chansma,
Dist- Patan, North Gujarat, India, Asia.
www.iphouseindia.com

First Publication: 15TH February, 2015

Copyright: Author

(c) Nilamben H. Sondarva

ISBN:- 978-15-08712-28-2

Price: Rs.750/- INDIA
$ 15 OUTSIDE INDIA

PUBLISHED BY

Hemchandracharya International Publishing House
HQ. At & Po. Chaveli., Ta- Chansma,
Dist- Patan, North Gujarat, India, Asia.
www.iphouseindia.com

Contents

CHAPTER 1
INTRODUCTION TO
PRODUCTION MANAGEMENT

INTRODUCTION :

Production management is the process, which combines and transforms various resources used in the production/operations subsystem of the organization into value added product/services in a controlled manner as per the policies of the organization. Therefore, it is that part of an organization, which is concerned with the transformation of a range of inputs into the required (products/services) having the requisite quality level. The set of interrelated management activities, which are involved in manufacturing certain products, is called as production management. If the same concept is extended to services management, then the corresponding set of management activities is called as operations management.

Production management is a process of planning, organizing, directing and controlling the activities of the production function. It combines and transforms various resources used in the production subsystem of the organization into value added product in a controlled manner as per the policies of the organization.

E.S. Buffa defines production management as, "Production management deals with decision making related to production processes so that the resulting goods or services are produced according to specifications, in the amount and by the schedule demanded and out of minimum cost."

PRODUCTION MANAGEMENT

Production management is a process of planning, organizing, directing and controlling the activities of the production function. It combines and transforms various resources used in the production subsystem of the organization into value added product in a controlled manner as per the policies of the organization. E.S. Buffa defines production management as, "Production management deals with decision making related to production processes so that the resulting goods or services are produced according to specifications, in the amount and by the schedule demanded and out of minimum cost."

Objectives of Production Management The objective of the production management is 'to produce goods services of right quality and quantity at the right time and right manufacturing cost'.

1. RIGHT QUALITY:

The quality of product is established based upon the customers needs. The right quality is not necessarily best quality. It is determined by the cost of the product and the technical characteristics as suited to the specific requirements.

2. RIGHT QUANTITY:

The manufacturing organization should produce the products in right number. If they are produced in excess of demand the capital will block up in the form of inventory and if the quantity is produced in short of demand, leads to shortage of products.

Production Management: it's Meaning and Important Aspects!

The function of production has assumed great significance as a Key function in almost all industrial/manufacturing undertakings. All other activities in such undertakings revolve around this key function. The activities of production are independent of the size of the enterprise.

In a small concern one person may be undertaking this function, whereas in large organisations this activity may be performed by many individuals or separate groups. The success or failure of an enterprise depends very much upon the extent of care and accuracy with which the production function is managed. Management of production function of an enterprise on scientific and rationalised lines is sure to help to achieve its objectives most successfully.

Meaning:

Production is the creation of goods and services. It is concerned with transforming the inputs in the form of raw materials, labour, machines, men and money into output i.e. goods and services with the help of certain production processes. Production function is the most important function in an organisation around which other activities of an enterprise (viz., marketing, financing, purchasing and personnel etc.) revolve. It is pertinent to note that production function should be managed in an efficient and effective manner for the achievement of the organisational goals.

In a departmental type of organisation, production management is concerned with carrying out the production function. Production management becomes the process of effectively planning and regulating the operations of that part of an enterprise which is responsible for actual transformation of raw materials into finished products.

Simply stated, production management is concerned with decision making relating to processes for producing goods and services in accordance with the predetermined specifications and standards by incurring minimum costs.

Important Aspects of production function:

Production function may be studied under the following headings:

1. Manufacturing function:

This function is concerned with the production of goods or making of products. Decisions such as selection of factory site, its location, design and layout, type of products to be produced, research, development and design of the product are included in manufacturing function.

2. Ancilliary function:

This function includes all the activities which support or smoothen production function. Ancilliary function is related to production planning and control, maintenance, purchasing, store-keeping and materials handling.

3. Advisory function:

This function helps in improving production function. It includes work study, method study, operational research, inspection and quality control.

Types of Production:

Some of the most important types of production are: (i) Job Production (ii) Batch production and (iii) Mass or flow production!

A production manager will have to choose most appropriate method for his enterprise. The final decision regarding any particular method of production is very much affected by the nature of the products and the quantity to be produced. Production methods may be broadly classified as Job Production, Batch production and Mass or Flow Production.

(i) Job Production:

Under this method peculiar, special or non-standardized products are produced in accordance with the orders received from the customers. As each product is non- standardized varying in size and nature, it requires separate job for production. The machines and equipment's are adjusted in such a manner so as to suit the requirements of a particular job.

Job production involves intermittent process as the work is carried as and when the order is received.

It consists of bringing together of material, parts and components in order to assemble and commission a single piece of equipment or product.

Ship building, dam construction, bridge building, book printing are some of the examples of job production. Third method of plant layout viz., Stationery Material Layout is suitable for job production.

Characteristics:

The job production possesses the following characteristics.

1. A large number of general purpose machines are required.

2. A large number of workers conversant with different jobs will have to be employed.

3. There can be some variations in production.

4. Some flexibility in financing is required because of variations in work load.

5. A large inventory of materials, parts and tools will be required.

6. The machines and equipment setting will have to be adjusted and readjusted to the manufacturing requirements.

7. The movement of materials through the process is intermittent.

Limitations:

Job production has the following limitations:

1. The economies of large scale production may not be attained because production is done in short-runs.

2. The demand is irregular for some products.

3. The use of labour and equipment may be an inefficient.

4. The scientific assessment of costs is difficult.

(ii) Batch production:

Batch production pertains to repetitive production. It refers to the production of goods, the quantity of which is known in advance.

It is that form of production where identical products are produced in batches on the basis of demand of customers' or of expected demand for products.

This method is generally similar to job production except the quantity of production. Instead of making one single product as in case of job production, a batch or group of products are produced at one time. It should be remembered here that one batch of products may not resemble with the next batch.

Under batch system of production the work is divided into operations and one operation is done at a time.

After completing the work on one operation it is passed on to the second operation and so on till the product is completed. Batch production can be explained with the help of an illustration. An enterprise wants to manufacture 20 electric motors.

The work will be divided into different operations. The first operation on all the motors will be completed in the first batch and then it will pass on to the next operation. The second group of operators will complete the second operation before the next and so on. Under job production the same operators will manufacture full machine and not one operation only.

Batch production can fetch the benefits of repetitive production to a large extent, if the batch is of a sufficient quantity. Thus batch production may be defined as the manufacture of a product in small or large batches or lots by series of operations, each operation being carried on the whole batch before any subsequent operation is operated.

This method is generally adopted in case of biscuit and confectionery and motor manufacturing, medicines, tinned food and hardware's like nuts and bolts etc.

The batch production method possesses the following characteristics:

1. The work is of repetitive nature.

2. There is a functional layout of various manufacturing processes.

3. One operation is carried out on whole batch and then is passed on to the next operation and so on.

4. Same type of machines is arranged at one place.

5. It is generally chosen where trade is seasonal or there is a need to produce great variety of goods.

(iii) Mass or flow production:

This method involves a continuous production of standardized products on a large scale. Under this method, production remains continuous in anticipation of future demand. Standardization is the basis of mass production. Standardized products are produced under this method by using standardized materials and equipment. There is a continuous or uninterrupted flow of production obtained by arranging the machines in a proper sequence of operations. Process layout is best suited method for mass production units.

Flow production is the manufacture of a product by a series of operations, each article going on to a succeeding operation as soon as possible. The manufacturing process is broken into separate operations.

The product completed at one operation is automatically passed on to the next till its completion. There is no time gap between the work done at one process and the starting at the next. The flow of production is continuous and progressive.

Characteristics:

The mass or flow production possesses the following characteristics.

1. The units flow from one operation point to another throughout the whole process.

2. There will be one type of machine for each process.

3. The products, tools, materials and methods are standardised.

4. Production is done in anticipation of demand.

5. Production volume is usually high.

6. Machine set ups remain unchanged for a considerable long period.

7. Any fault in flow of production is immediately corrected otherwise it will stop the whole production process.

Suitability of flow/mass production:

1. There must be continuity in demand for the product.

2. The products, materials and equipments must be standardised because the flow of line is inflexible.

3. The operations should be well defined.

4. It should be possible to maintain certain quality standards.

5. It should be possible to find time taken at each operation so that flow of work is standardised.

6. The process of stages of production should be continuous.

Advantages of mass production:

A properly planned flow production method, results in the following advantages:

1. The product is standardised and any deviation in quality etc. is detected at the spot.

2. There will be accuracy in product design and quality.

3. It will help in reducing direct labour cost.

4. There will be no need of work-in-progress because products will automatically pass on from operation to operation.

5. Since flow of work is simplified there will be lesser need for control.

6. A weakness in any operation comes to the notice immediately.

7. There may not be any need of keeping work-in-progress, hence storage cost is reduced.

SCOPE OF PRODUCTION AND OPERATIONS MANAGEMENT

Production and operations management concern with the conversion of inputs into outputs, using physical resources, so as to provide the desired utilities to the customer while meeting the other organizational objectives of effectiveness, efficiency and adoptability. It distinguishes itself from other functions such as personnel, marketing, finance, etc., by its primary concern for 'conversion by using physical resources.'

Following are the activities which are listed under production and operations management functions:

1. Location of facilities
2. Plant layouts and material handling
3. Product design
4. Process design
5. Production and planning control
6. Quality control
7. Materials management
8. Maintenance management.

LOCATION OF FACILITIES:

Location of facilities for operations is a long-term capacity decision which involves a long term commitment about the geographically static factors that affect a business organization. It is an important strategic level decision-making for an organization. It deals with the questions such as 'where our main operations should be based?'

The selection of location is a key-decision as large investment is made in building plant and machinery. An improper location of plant may lead to waste of all the investments made in plant and machinery equipments. Hence, location of plant should be based on the company's expansion plan and policy, diversification plan for the products, changing sources of raw materials and many other factors. The purpose of the location study is to find the optimal location that will results in the greatest advantage to the organization.

PLANT LAYOUT AND MATERIAL HANDLING :

Plant layout refers to the physical arrangement of facilities. It is the configuration of departments, work centres and equipment in the conversion process. The overall objective of the plant layout is to design a physical arrangement that meets the required output quality and quantity most economically.

According to James Moore, "Plant layout is a plan of an optimum arrangement of facilities including personnel, operating equipment, storage space, material handling equipments and all other supporting services along with the design of best structure to contain all these facilities".

'Material Handling' refers to the 'moving of materials from the store room to the machine and from one machine to the next during the process of manufacture'. It is also defined as the 'art and science of moving, packing and storing of products in any form'. It is a specialised activity for a modern manufacturing concern, with 50 to 75% of the cost of production.

This cost can be reduced by proper section, operation and maintenance of material handling devices. Material handling devices increases the output, improves quality, speeds up the deliveries and decreases the cost of production. Hence, material handling is a prime consideration in the designing new plant and several existing plants.

PRODUCT DESIGN :

Product design deals with conversion of ideas into reality. Every business organization have to design, develop and introduce new products as a survival and growth strategy. Developing the new products and launching them in the market is the biggest challenge faced by the organizations. The entire process of need identification to physical manufactures of product involves three functions: marketing, product development, manufacturing. Product development translates the needs of customers given by marketing into technical specifications and designing the various features into the product to these specifications.

Manufacturing has the responsibility of selecting the processes by which the product can be manufactured. Product design and development provides link between marketing, customer needs and expectations and the activities required to manufacture the product.

PROCESS DESIGN:

Process design is a macroscopic decision-making of an overall process route for converting the raw material into finished goods. These decisions encompass the selection of a process, choice of technology, process flow analysis and layout of the facilities. Hence, the important decisions in process design are to analyse the workflow for converting raw material into finished product and to select the workstation for each included in the workflow.

PRODUCTION PLANNING AND CONTROL :

Production planning and control can be defined as the process of planning the production in advance, setting the exact route of each item, fixing the starting and finishing dates for each item, to give production orders to shops and to follow up the progress of products according to orders.

The principle of production planning and control lies in the statement 'First Plan Your Work and then Work on Your Plan'. Main functions of production planning and control includes planning, routing, scheduling, dispatching and follow-up. Planning is deciding in advance what to do, how to do it, when to do it and who is to do it.

Planning bridges the gap from where we are, to where we want to go. It makes it possible for things to occur which would not otherwise happen. Routing may be defined as the selection of path which each part of the product will follow, which being transformed from raw material to finished products.

Steps in Production Planning and Control

According to the British Standards Institute, there are four stages, steps, techniques or essentials in the process of production planning and control.

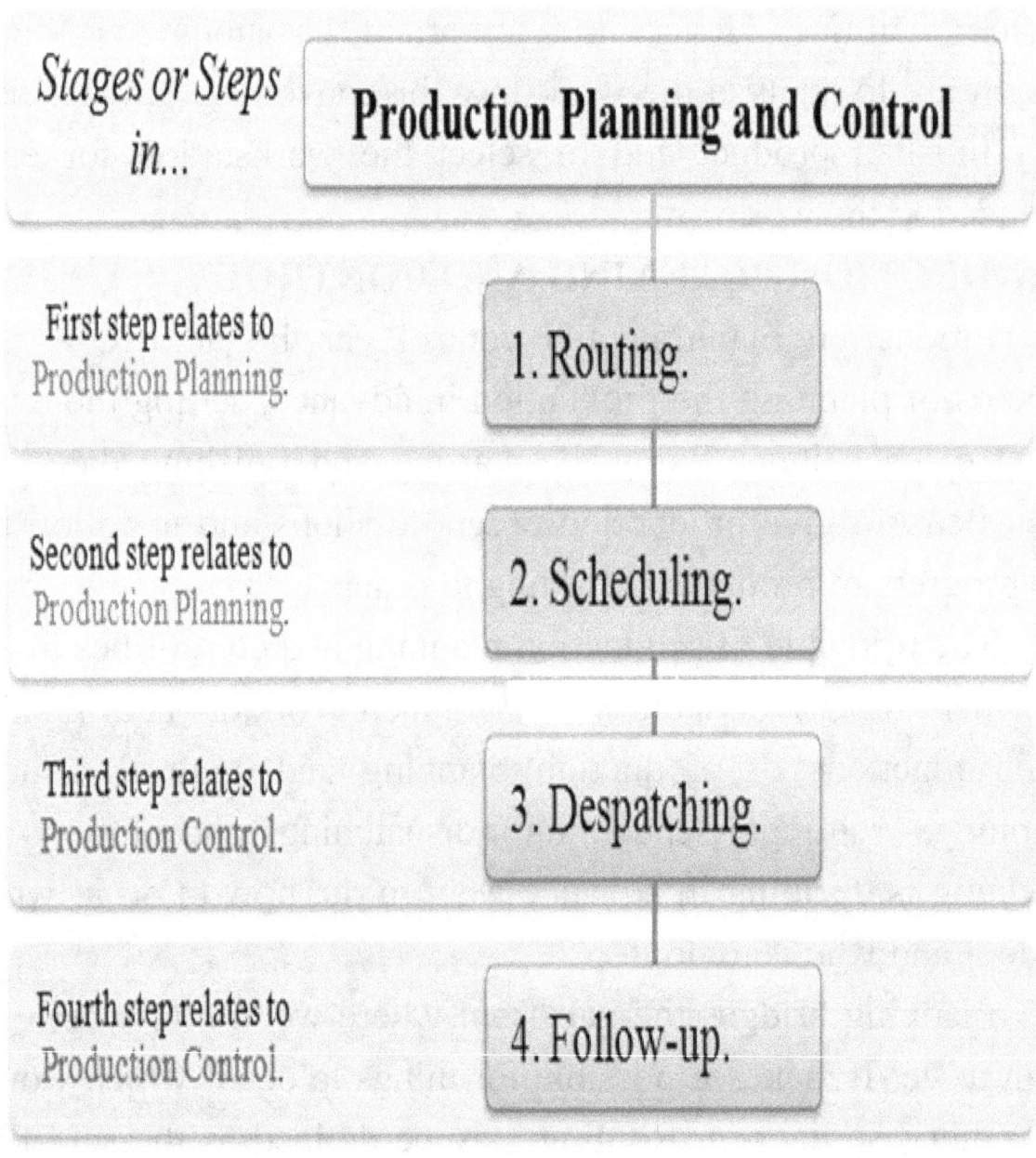

The four stages or steps in production planning and control are:

➢ Routing

➢ Scheduling

➢ Dispatching

➢ Follow-up

Initial two steps i.e. Routing and Scheduling, relate to production planning. Last two steps i.e. Dispatching and Follow-up, relate to production control.

Now let's continue our discussion further to understand each step in detail.

1. Routing

Routing is the first step in production planning and control. Routing can be defined as the process of deciding the path (route) of work and the sequence of operations. Routing fixes in advance: The quantity and quality of the product. The men, machines, materials, etc. to be used. The type, number and sequence of manufacturing operations, and The place of production.

In short, routing determines 'What', 'How much', 'With which', 'How' and 'Where' to produce. Routing may be either very simple or complex. This depends upon the nature of production. In a continuous production, it is automatic, i.e. it is very simple. However, in a job order, it is very complex. Routing is affected by the human factor. Therefore, it should recognize human needs, desires and expectations. It is also affected by plant-layout, characteristics of the equipment, etc. The main objective of routing is to determine (fix) the best and cheapest sequence of operations and to ensure that this sequence is followed in the factory.

Routing gives a very systematic method of converting raw-materials into finished goods. It leads to smooth and efficient work. It leads to optimum utilization of resources; namely, men, machines, materials, etc. It leads to division of labor. It ensures a continuous flow of materials without any backtracking. It saves time and space. It makes the work easy for the production engineers and foremen. It has a great influence on design of factory's building and installed machines. So, routing is an important step in production planning and control.

2. Scheduling

Scheduling is the second step in production planning and control. It comes after routing. Scheduling means to:

Fix the amount of work to do. Arrange the different manufacturing operations in order of priority. Fix the starting and completing, date and time, for each operation. Scheduling is also done for materials, parts, machines, etc.

So, it is like a time-table of production. It is similar to the time-table, prepared by the railways. Time element is given special importance in scheduling. There are different types of schedules; namely, Master schedule, Operation schedule and Daily schedule.

Scheduling helps to make optimum use of time. It sees that each piece of work is started and completed at a certain predetermined time. It helps to complete the job systematically and in time. It brings time coordination in production planning. All this helps to deliver the goods to the customers in time. It also eliminates the idle capacity. It keeps labor continuously employed.

So, scheduling is an important step in production planning and control. It is essential in a factory, where many products are produced at the same time.

3. Dispatching

Dispatching is the third step in production planning and control. It is the action, doing or implementation stage. It comes after routing and scheduling.

Dispatching means starting the process of production. It provides the necessary authority to start the work. It is based on route-sheets and schedule sheets.

Dispatching includes the following: Issue of materials, tools, fixtures, etc., which are necessary for actual production. Issue of orders, instructions, drawings, etc. for starting the work. Maintaining proper records of the starting and completing each job on time. Moving the work from one process to another as per the schedule. Starting the control procedure. Recording the idle time of machines.

Dispatching may be either centralized or decentralized:

Under centralized dispatching, orders are issued directly by a centralized authority. Under decentralized dispatching, orders are issued by the concerned department.

4. Follow-up

Follow-up or Expediting is the last step in production planning and control. It is a controlling device. It is concerned with evaluation of the results.

Follow-up finds out and removes the defects, delays, limitations, bottlenecks, loopholes, etc. in the production process. It measures the actual performance and compares it to the expected performance. It maintains proper records of work, delays and bottlenecks. Such records are used in future to control production.

Follow-up is performed by 'Expediters' or 'Stock Chasers'. Follow-up is necessary when production decreases even when there is proper routing and scheduling. Production may be disturbed due to break-downs of machinery, failure of power, shortage of materials, strikes, absenteeism, etc.

Follow-up removes these difficulties and allows a smooth production.

Production Control: Definition, Necessity, Objectives and Levels

Definition of Production Control:

There is lot of disagreement between different experts of management regarding the meaning of production control. The term itself appears to be quite confusing and misleading. In literary sense control means action to check/regulate.

In the opinion of Mary Gushing Niles, "Control is maintaining a balance in activities towards a goal or set of goals evolved during production planning." Planning only outlines some course of action whereas control is an execution process involving standardisation, evaluation and corrective functions.

According to Fayol, "Control consists in verifying whether everything occurs in conformity with the adopted plan and established principles. The objective of control is to point out weaknesses and shortcomings, if any, in order to rectify them and prevent recurrence.

It operates on everything viz. material, equipment, men, operations etc. For control to be effective, it must be applied within reasonable time and be followed-up sanctions."

Thus production control is some scientific procedure to regulate an orderly flow of material and co-ordinate various production operations to accomplish the objective of producing desired item. In right quantity of desired quality at the required time by the best and the cheapest method i.e., to attain highest efficiency in production.

Alternately, production control is the function of management which plans, directs and controls the material supply and processing activities of an enterprise; so that specified products are produced by specified methods to meet an approved sales programme. It ensures that the activities are carried in such a way that the available labour and capital are used in the best possible way.

Necessity of Production Control:

Production process of an enterprise is a system consisting of material, labour and equipment combined together by some dependence imposed by operations. Input factors in the process are always uncontrollable. The controller of a production process tries to control the output so that it is in conformity with the target set by the marketing department.

Production control tries to channelise the manufacturing process in such a manner that goods and services are produced according to the requirements of the consumer, i.e., of right quality, shape and quantity at the desired time.

In the present era of cut-throat competition, production control is a boon for an enterprise. It tries to take corrective measures whenever thoro is some deviation from the planned strategy. Goetz has rightly said that "Management planning seeks consistent, integrated and articulated programmes." Production control aims to fulfill these needs.

In the report on the elimination of waste in industry. President Noover's committee states that "Production control is the hallmark of production efficiency., it is a necessity and not a luxury; a profitable investment and not an expense."

Objectives of Production Control:

The success of an enterprise greatly depends on the performance of its production control department.

The production control department generally has to perform the following functions:

(i) Provision of raw material, equipment, machines and labour.

(ii) To organise production schedule in conformity with the demand forecast.

(iii) The resources are used in the best possible manner in such a way that the cost of production is minimised and delivery date is maintained.

(iv) Determination of economic production runs with a view to reduce setup costs.

(v) Proper co-ordination of the operations of various sections/departments responsible for production.

(vi) To ensure regular and timely supply of raw material at the desired place and of prescribed quality and quantity to avoid delays in production.

(vii) To perform inspection of semi-finished and finished goods and use quality control techniques to ascertain that the produced items are of required specifications.

(viii) It is also responsible for product design and development.

Thus, the fundamental objective of production control is to regulate and control the various operations of production process in such a way that orderly flow of material is ensured at different stages of the production and the items are produced of right quality in right quantity at the right time with minimum efforts and cost.

Levels of Production Control:

Production Control starts with some particular goal and formulation of some general strategy for the accomplishment of desired objectives. There are three levels of production control namely programming, ordering and dispatching. Programming plans the output of products for the factory as a whole.

Ordering plans the output of components from the suppliers and processing departments. Dispatching considers each processing department in turn and plans the output from the machine, tools and other work centres so as to complete the orders by due date.

Importance of Production Planning and Control

For efficient, effective and economical operation in a manufacturing unit of an organization, it is essential to integrate the production planning and control system. Production planning and subsequent production control follow adaption of product design and finalization of a production process. Production planning is an activity that is performed before the actual production process takes place. It involves determining the schedule of production, sequence of operations, economic batch quantities, and also the dispatching priorities for sequencing of jobs. Production control is mainly involved in implementing production schedules and is the corollary to short-term production planning or scheduling.

Production control includes initiating production, dispatching items, progressing and then finally reporting back to production planning. In general terms, production planning means planning of the work to be done later and production control refers to working out or the implementation of the plan.

So, the system of production planning and control serves as the nervous system of a plant. It is a co- ordinating agency which co-ordinate the activities of engineering, purchasing, production, selling and stock control departments. An efficient system of production planning and control helps in providing better and more economic goods to customers at lower investment. It is essential in all plants irrespective of their nature and size.

The importance of production planning and control are summarized below:

- **Better Service to Customers:** Production planning and control, through proper scheduling and expediting of work, helps in providing better services to customers is terms of better quality of goods at reasonable prices as per promised delivery dates. Delivery in time and proper quality, both help in winning the confidence of customers, improving relations with customers and promoting profitable repeat orders.

- **Fewer Rush Orders :** In an organization, where there is effective system of production planning and control, production, operations move smoothly as per original planning and matching with the promised delivery dates.

Consequently, there will be fewer rush orders in the plant and less overtime than, in the same industry, without adequate production planning and control.

- **Better Control of Inventory :** A sound system of production planning and control helps inmaintaining inventory at proper levels and, thereby, minimizing investment in inventory. It requires lower inventory of work-in-progress and less finished stock to give efficient service to customers. It also helps in exercising better control over raw-material inventory, which contributes to more effective purchasing.

- **More Effective Use of Equipment :** An efficient system of production planning and control makes for the most effective use of equipment.

  It provides information to the management on regular basis pertaining to the present position of all orders in process, equipment and personnel requirements for next few weeks. The workers can be communicated well in advance if any retrenchment, lay-offs, transfer, etc. is likely to come about. Also, unnecessary purchases of equipment and materials can be avoided. Thus, it is possible to ensure proper utilization of equipment and other resources.

- **Reduced Idle Time :** Production planning and control helps in reducing idle time i.e. loss of time by workers waiting for materials and other facilities; because ensures that materials and other facilities are available to the workers in time as per the production schedule. Consequently, less man-hours are lost, which has a positive impact on the cost of production.

- **Improved Plant Morale** : An effective system of production planning and control co-ordinates the activities of all the departments involved in the production activity. It ensures even flow of work and avoids rush orders. It maintains healthy working conditions in the plant thus, there is improve plant morale as a by-product.

- **Good public image**: A proper system of production planning and control is helpful in keeping systematized operations in an organization. Such an organization is in a position to meet its orders in time to the satisfaction of its customers. Customers satisfaction leads to increased sales, increased profits, industrial harmony and ultimately good public image of the enterprise .

- **Lower capital requirements**: Under a sound system of production planning and control, everything relating to production is planned well in advance of operations. Where, when and what is required in the form of input is known before the actual production process starts. Inputs are made available as per schedule which ensures even flow of production without any bottlenecks. Facilities are used more effectively and inventory levels are kept as per schedule neither more nor less. Thus, production planning and control helps, in minimizing capital investment in equipment and inventories.

CHAPTER 2
PURCHASING

Purchasing refers to a business or organization attempting to acquiring goods or services to accomplish the goals of its enterprise. Though there are several organizations that attempt to set standards in the purchasing process, processes can vary greatly between organizations. Typically the word "purchasing" is not used interchangeably with the word "procurement", since procurement typically includes expediting, supplier quality, and transportation and logistics (T&L) in addition to purchasing.

Purchasing managers/directors, and procurement managers/directors guide the organization's acquisition procedures and standards. Most organizations use a three-way check as the foundation of their purchasing programs. This involves three departments in the organization completing separate parts of the acquisition process. The three departments do not all report to the same senior manager, to prevent unethical practices and lend credibility to the process. These departments can be purchasing, receiving and accounts payable; or engineering, purchasing and accounts payable; or a plant manager, purchasing and accounts payable. Combinations can vary significantly, but a purchasing department and accounts payable are usually two of the three departments involved.

When the receiving department is not involved, it is typically called a two-way check or two-way purchase order. In this situation, the purchasing department issues the purchase order receipt not required. When an invoice arrives against the order, the accounts payable department will then go directly to the requestor of the purchase order to verify that the goods or services were received. This is typically what is done for goods and services that will bypass the receiving department. A few examples are software delivered electronically, NRE work (non-reoccurring engineering services), consulting hours, etc.

Historically, the purchasing department issued purchase orders for supplies, services, equipment, and raw materials. Then, in an effort to decrease the administrative costs associated with the repetitive ordering of basic consumable items, "blanket" or "master" agreements were put into place. These types of agreements typically have a longer duration and increased scope to maximize the quantities of scale concept. When additional supplies were required, a simple release would be issued to the supplier to provide the goods or services.

Another method of decreasing administrative costs associated with repetitive contracts for common material, is the use of company credit cards, also known as "Purchasing Cards" or simply "P-Cards". P-card programs vary, but all of them have internal checks and audits to ensure appropriate use. Purchasing managers realized once contracts for the low dollar value consumables are in place, procurement can take a smaller role in the operation and use of the contracts. There is still oversight in the forms of audits and monthly statement reviews, but most of their time is now available to negotiate major purchases and setting up of other long term contracts. These contracts are typically renewable annually.

This trend away from the daily procurement function (tactical purchasing) resulted in several changes in the industry. The first was the reduction of personnel.

There was no need for the army of clerks processing orders for individual parts as in the past. Another change was the focus on negotiating contracts and procurement of large capital equipment. Both of these functions permitted purchasing departments to make the biggest financial contribution to the organization. A new terms and job title emerged – Strategic sourcing and Sourcing Managers. These professionals not only focused on the bidding process and negotiating with suppliers, but the entire supply function. In these roles they were able to add value and maximize savings for organizations.

This value was manifested in lower inventories, less personnel, and getting the end product to the organization's consumer quicker. Purchasing manager's success in these roles resulted in new assignments outside to the traditional purchasing function – logistics, materials management, distribution, and warehousing. More and more purchasing managers were becoming Supply Chain Managers handling additional functions of their organizations operation. Purchasing managers were not the only ones to become Supply Chain Managers.

Logistic managers, material managers, distribution managers, etc. all rose the broader function and some had responsibility for the purchasing functions now.

In accounting, purchases is the amount of goods a company bought throughout this year. It also refers to information as to the kind, quality, quantity, and cost of goods bought that should be maintained. They are added to inventory.

Purchases are offset by Purchase Discounts and Purchase Returns and Allowances. When it should be added depends on the Free On Board (FOB) policy of the trade. For the purchaser, this new inventory is added on shipment if the policy was FOB shipping point, and the seller remove this item from its inventory. On the other hand, the purchaser added this inventory on receipt if the policy was FOB destination, and the seller remove this item from its inventory when it was delivered.

Goods bought for the purpose other than direct selling, such as for Research and Development, are added to inventory and allocated to Research and Development expense as they are used. On a side note, equipments bought for Research and Development are not added to inventory, but are capitalized as assets.

Principles of Scientific Purchasing

Purchasing is one of the integral aspects of material management. "Purchasing materials of right quality, right quantity at right time from right source at right price and taking delivery at right place are the six elements or principles of scientific purchasing." These principles or elements answer the blowing questions relating to purchasing:

What to purchase? -> Right quality

When to purchase? -> Right time

How much to purchase? -> Right quantity

From where to purchase? -> Right source

At what rate? -> Right price

At what place to receive? -> Right place

The above Six Rights are the Six Rights of scientific purchasing.

Procedure of Purchasing

Purchasing is a very important work is an organisation. The basic function of the purchase department is to purchase the right quality of material from the right source, at the right price and at the right time. The purchase department follows the following procedure for-purchasing necessary materials:

A. Receiving purchase requisitions

B. Determining the sources of supply and selecting the suppliers.

C. Preparing and placing purchase order

D. Follow up of purchase order

E. receiving and inspecting purchase order

F. Checking and passing bills for payment.

Receiving Purchase Requisitions

The purchase department does not on its own initiate any action for purchase of j materials.

The store- keeper takes initiative of preparing the purchase requisition for regular supply of materials.

The Planning and Production Department prepares it for j special materials meant of special or irregular jobs. A special type of purchase requisition is called 'Bill of Material'.

The plant engineer prepares it for procurement j of capital expenditure goods (machineries) and maintenance materials. The Heads of j Departments, prepare it for indirect materials.

The purchase requisition is a formal request made to the purchase manager arrange for the purchase of materials described in the purchase requisition. Purchase requisition is also called as "Indent for materials".

It is a statement that contains alit of material and a request to purchase them. It serves as a basis for purchasing their materials when it is signed by authorized persons. Thus purchase requisition serves the j following two purposes:

(i) It authorizes the purchase department to make a purchase, and

(ii) It provides a written proof showing specification, quantity and date of requisite of materials and supplies.

The requisition gives clearly all information that is required for initiation off purchase.

Contents:

Purchase requisition contains the following information:

(a) Name and exact description of materials wanted

(b) Quantity required

(c) Date on which materials are required

(d) Statement of need

(e) The place of delivery

(f) Signature of the person initiating requisition

The purchase requisition is usually prepared in triplicate and different shade colors. The original is sent to purchase department, the duplicate is sent to production Department and triplicate is retained in the department that initiates.

Determining the sources of supply and selecting the supplier

On receiving the purchase requisition the sources of supply are to be explored. The important sources of supply of materials are: (1) Price list (2) Advertisement (3) Trade Directories (4) Telephone directory (5) Purchase periodicals (6) News paper and magazine (7) Exhibition and Trade shows (8) Market survey (9) Tenders (10) Past experience of purchase manager etc.

In case there is more than one supplier dealing with materials, the purchase manager has to select the best supplier with whom he has confidence.

The selection of such supplier is decided by issuing a 'tender' taking into account quality of materials, ability to deliver the material, the better terms of sale, lowest price, manufacturing capacity, financial condition of supplier, etc.

A tender is a written letter or an advertisement given in newspaper inviting the prospective suppliers to quote their lowest price and other terms and conditions of sale, the different methods of obtaining tenders are:

(i) Open Tender (i.e. by open advertisement),

(ii) Limited Tender (i.e. by direct invitation to limited number of firms or companies),

(iii) Single Tender (i.e. by inviting one company only).

The request for quotation should contain the following:

(1) Quantity to be ordered,

(2) Name and full specification of materials,

(3) Place of delivery of material and

(4) Other terms and conditions of sale

The sealed quotations are opened before the responsible officer after the expiry of last date of submission. The purchase manager determines the lowest quotation by preparing a comparative statement.

Then the supplier is selected to whom purchase order is to be issued. For each type of material, a separate comparative statement is prepared. It may be noted that only lowest price quoted is not the sufficient criteria to select a supplier. Other factors like quality of material, time of delivery, trade discount, credit facility, transportation cost, terms of payment, dependability of the supplier, etc have also to be considered.

Purchase Order

After selecting the supplier, purchase department prepares an order for supply of stores. A purchase order is thus a request made by purchaser to a supplier to supply certain goods of requisite quantity and quality at the terms and conditions agreed upon, It is the evidence of a contract between the buyer and the supplier that binds both o them to the terms under which the order is placed. The purchase order should be carefully drafted so as to avoid future misunderstanding and minimize future correspondence. The purchase order should include the following particulars:

(a) Name of the buying concern, serial number and date of order.

(b) Name and address of supplier.

(c) Full description of material and quantity.

(d) Date and place of delivery.

(e) Price, discount and terms of payment.

(f) Packing and dispatching instructions.

(g) Signature of purchase officer.

A Specimen of Purchase Order is given below:

The number of copies of purchase order to be made depends on the size organisation. Accordingly three to five copies are made. If five copies are made, it possible use may be as follows:

The original copy is sent to supplier

One copy is sent to receiving department.

One copy is sent to accounting department.

One copy is sent to the initiating department.

The last copy is retained by purchase department for future reference.

Following up of Purchase Order

To ensure timely supply of materials, so that production process is interrupted, there should be regular follow up. For that following steps may be taken:

(i) Obtaining acknowledgement of purchase order.

(ii) Obtaining written confirmation from the supplier about giving deliver within the specified time.

(iii) Reminding the supplier over phone and taking remedial measures I delayed delivery.

Receiving and Inspecting Materials

It is very essential to receive and inspect materials so as to ensure that the exact quantity and quality of materials are being supplied by supplier. In large organisation a separate Receipt and Inspection Department is set up and receiving clerk's are charge of receiving materials.

But in small organisation, the work of receiving the go may be entrusted to the storekeeper. Supplier dispatches the goods along Delivery Chelan in duplicate. Delivery Chelan shows the details of goods, if description, quantity, etc. Receiving officer acknowledges the Delivery Chelan receiving the delivery of goods signs it and sends back the duplicate copy to the supplier. The functions of receipt and inspection department are:

(i) To check the incoming materials with purchase order.

(ii) To record the receipt of materials.

(iii) To inform the storekeeper about the receipt of materials.

(iv) To inform the purchase manager about the shortage or defective materials.

(v) To deliver the materials either to the department where it is required or to the store room.

After the goods have been inspected and checked, the goods receiving clerk enters the details of goods received in a Goods Received Note.

Five copies of the note should be prepared.

(a) One copy is sent to Purchase Department.

(b) One copy is sent to Accounting Department.

(c) One copy is sent to Store Keeper.

(d) One copy is sent to the department which initiated the purchase requisition.

(e) One copy is retained in the Receiving Department.

Checking and Passing the Bills for Payment

This is the last step in the purchase procedure. The invoice is checked with the purchase order and the material received report.

The rates and terms of invoice are compared with those of purchase order. The arithmetical accuracy is also checked. When there is any discrepancy or defect, the same is brought to the notice of supplier.

Finally when everything is in order, the invoice is approved by the purchase manager and sent to Accounts Department for payment.

Objectives of Purchasing

Purchasing is an important and inevitable activity of any business or non-trading activities. Progressive organizations recognize it as an important function and organize a separate purchase department to look after the purchase function. The objectives of the purchase function must be spelt out clearly for the justification of its independent existence. Moreover, purchasing being the part of the total management activity must see that its objectives are in conformity with the overall objectives of the organization. Identification of objectives encourages the imaginative personnel to accelerate their efforts in attaining them efficiently and economically.

Objectives are set by the head of the purchasing department either in consultation with the top management or on the line of the broad policies outlined by the top management.

The objectives of the purchase department can be outlined as under:

To avail the materials, supplies and equipment at the minimum possible costs: These are the basic inputs in the manufacturing operations. The minimization of the input cost increases the productivity and resultant profitability of the operations.

To ensure the continuous flow of production: Purchasing department helps in ensuring the interrupted production flow through continuous supply of raw material, components, supplies, tools etc. and good equipment with repair and maintenance services.

To increase the asset turnover: the efforts of purchase department result in formation of fixed assets and maintenance of a certain level of investments in inventories. The investments in fixed assets and also in the inventories should be kept at minimum in relation to the corresponding volume of sales. This will increase the turnover of the assets and thus the profitability of the company will get enhanced.

To develop the alternate sources of supply: Exploration of alternate sources of supply of materials increases the bargaining ability of the buyer, minimization of cost of materials and increases the ability to meet the emergencies.

To established and maintain the good relations with the suppliers: Maintenance of good relations with the supplier helps in evolving a favorable image in the business circles. Such relations are always beneficial to the buyer in terms of changing of reasonable price, preferential allocation of materials in case of material shortages, intimation about forthcoming shortages, information about the newly developed substitute, prolonged payments in case of temporary liquidity crisis etc.

To achieve maximum integration with other departments of the company: The purchase function is related with the following other departments of the company:

i) Production department regarding the material specification, flow of materials, suggested supplies for certain items etc.

ii) Engineering department for the purchase of tools, machines and equipment.

iii) Marketing department regarding the forecast sales and its impact on procurement of materials, impact of quality of inputs on quality of outputs and sales.

iv) Finance department for the purpose of maintaining levels of materials, pledging and hypothecating the materials for meeting working capital needs, tapping the quantity discount, scheduling the investments in capital assets such as materials and equipment.

v) Personnel department for the purpose of manning and developing the personnel of purchase department, maintaining the vendor relationships etc.

To train and develop the personnel: Purchasing department is manned with varied types of personnel. The company should try to build the imaginative employees force through training and development. This will ensure management succession and a contended workforce who are provided with an opportunity to fulfill their aspirations through promotions on higher positions.

Efficient record keeping and management reporting: paper processing is inherent in the purchase function. Such paper processing should be standardized so that the record keeping is facilitated.

The periodic to the management about the purchase activities is also one of the important activities which justifies the independent existence of purchase department. The management is interested in knowing the following aspects of the purchase functions which provides them the valuable data for shaping certain important policies:

1. To know the volume and value of the purchase broken into raw materials, supplies, pares, components, machines and equipment.

2. To know the departmental cost of the purchase department according to the important heads of expenditure.

3. Analysis of the work performed in the purchase departments.

4. Information about the cash discount and quantity discount earned and lost.

5. The trend about the price changes in foreseeable future and its impact on the cost of inventories.

6. The predictions about the availability of materials and the development of the strategy against such predictions.

7. The information about the new materials and processes which may reduce the manufacturing costs.

8. Exploration of new sources of supply.

Concept And Meaning of Centralized Purchasing,Its Advantages And Disadvantages

Concept And Meaning of Centralized Purchasing

Centralized purchasing refers to the purchase of materials by a single purchase department. This department is headed and managed by a purchasing manager. Under centralized purchasing, all purchases made by the purchase department to avoid duplication, overlapping and the non-uniform procurement. A company has to follow the centralized purchasing of materials for ensuring proper materials control as well as efficient store keeping. Under this system, the purchasing department purchases the required materials for all the departments and branches of the company.

Centralizing purchasing becomes increasingly more important the larger a small business grows. Most importantly, a decentralized purchasing structure in which individual departments are responsible for their own purchasing activities is often both costly and inefficient. In contrast, a centralized organizational and management structure reduces purchasing costs and creates a more efficient purchasing department.

Advantages and disadvantages of Centralized Purchasing

The centralized purchasing avails the following advantages:
1) As the duplication of efforts in buying function is eliminated, its cost will be relatively less and it will be managed efficiently
2) The Manager of manufacturing departments, departmental

heads and office managers are relieved from the responsibility of purchasing their own requirements. They can concentrate in their assigned areas of activities in a better way.

3) It is possible to tap the advantage of the specialized skill of the buying staff.

4) Bulk buying strengthens the bargaining position of the buyer. Moreover, the advantage of the quantity discount can be tapped. Direct contact with the suppliers will be possible which will eliminate the link of the intermediaries.

5) It enables to develop and maintain good relations with the suppliers. Moreover, it facilitates the supplier to maintain relations with few buyers and thus it enables him to pass over some benefits on buyers.

6) It will enable the purchase of standardized items through standardized procedure.

7) It will reduce the inventory carrying costs. The minimum level of inventory are not maintained at different centers but at centralized center which reduce investments in inventories along with the other incidental storing costs. The central buying staff manages the stock levels, recording material usage, lead time and prices effectively.

8) The receiving of large supply through consolidated orders reduces the transport cost per unit.

9) The cost of order processing such as order placing, receiving, inspection, accounts etc are reduced substantially due to few orders of large quantities.

10) As the responsibility center is fixed on one departmental head, the shifting of responsibility for wrong decisions is eliminated.

11) The inter-section requirements of the materials can be easily adjusted. Scarce materials can be allocated according to the economical advantage.

Disadvantages

The centralized purchasing suffers from the following limitations:

1) The specific requirements of the individual items may not be attended successfully. At times, it may result in absence of matching of mind between the needy section and the buying section resulting in wrong buying.

2) The centralized standard procedure may result in delays in receiving the materials.

3) It is likely that the centralized buying staff may not be expert in buying varied types of items.

4) In case of multi-plant units located at distant places and receiving their requirements from centralized storing, it may not be possible to tap the local resources. However, this situation can be handled effectively authorizing the regional purchase agent to make local purchases if they involve cost advantage.

5) It adversely affects the employee morale. It can be concluded that the company should centralize all policy matters, the purchase of major raw materials and capital equipment should

be made by the head office, while the individual divisions should be allowed to make their own purchases in accordance with the policies established by central office. If the company adopts the "profit center decentralized" set up the decentralized should be made accordingly.

Purchasing manual: The purchasing manual is an important means of effective purchasing. It outlines the policies and procedures to be followed by the purchasing personnel. It contains the approved statement of policies and thus provides standing answer to recurring questions.

Purchasing manual sometimes becomes a source of irritation and conflict. Many purchasing managers consider it to restrictive. In fact such situations can be eliminated if the following aspects are considered while preparing the manual:

1) The purchase authorities should be clearly defined.

2) It should clarify the relationship with other departments.

3) The co-operation of the personnel should be sought while preparing the manual.

4) It should be drafted clearly.

5) The policies and procedures should be segregated. Generally, policies are of permanent nature while procedures are subject of frequent changes.

Purchasing manual is an important tool for managing the purchase function efficiently. It is not only useful to the large organization, but is required in small organizations as well. In the large organization, the purchase function is relatively complex and can be eased with the help of the purchasing manual. In the small organization, it is essentially required because in such organization, purchasing function becomes a one man show and the absence of such key man may paralyze the purchase activity. Purchasing manual attempts to reduce such over dependence of one man.

Decentralisation: Meaning, Advantages and Disadvantages of Decentralisation

Meaning:

Decentralisation can be viewed as an extension of delegation.

When a part of the work is entrusted to others, it is known as delegation. Decentralisation extends to the lowest level of the organisation.

A few definitions are given below:

1. "Decentralisation refers to tire systematic effort to delegate to the lowest levels all authority except that which can only be exercised at central points." —Louis A. Allen

2. "Decentralisation means the division of a group of functions and activities into relatively autonomous units with overall authority and responsibility for their operation delegate to timd of cacti unit.'—Earl. P. Strong

3. "Decentralisation is simply a matter of dividing up the managerial work and assigning specific duties to the various executive skills."

—Newman, summer and Wairen

Thus, decentralisation is concerned with the decentralisation of decision-making authority to the lower levels in managerial hierarchy.

Degree of Decentralisation:

The degree of decentralisation is determined by:

(a) Nature of the authority delegated,

(b) How far down in the organisation it is delegated,

(c) How consistently it is delegated.

So, the degree of decentralisation is determined by the authority given. For example, manager A in a company is given the authority to buy certain material worth Rs. 1500 whereas manager B is allowed to do similar type of work to the extent of Rs. 4500.

It is clear that the degree of decentralisation is less in case of A. Similarly decisions about the matters referred, measure the degree of decentralisation depending upon the power to take decisions vested in an officer without the need of getting consent of somebody else.

Advantages of Decentralisation:

1. Reduces the burden on top executives:

Decentralisation relieves the top executives of the burden of performing various functions. Centralisation of authority puts the whole responsibility on the shoulders of an executive and his immediate group.

This reduces the time at the disposal of top executives who should concentrate on other important managerial functions. So, the only way to lessen their burden is to decentralise the decision-making power to the subordinates.

2. Facilitates diversification:

Under decentralization, the diversification of products, activites and markets etc., is facilitated. A centralised enterprise with the concentration of authority at the top will find it difficult and complex to diversify its activities and start the additional lines of manufacture or distribution.

3. To provide product and market emphasis:

A product loses its market when new products appear in the market on account of innovations or changes in the customers demand. In such cases authority is decentralised to the regional units to render instant service taking into account the price, quality, delivery, novelty, etc.

4. Executive Development:

When the authority is decentralised, executives in the organisation will get the opportunity to develop their talents by taking initiative which will also make them ready for managerial positions. The growth of the company greatly depends on the talented executives.

5. It promotes motivation:

To quote Louis A. Allen, "Decentralisation stimulates the formation of small cohesive groups. Since local managers are given a large degree of authority and local autonomy, they tend to weld their people into closely knit integrated groups." This improves the morale of employees as they get involved in decision-making process.

6. Better control and supervision:

Decentralisation ensures better control and supervision as the subordinates at the lowest levels will have the authority to make independent decisions. As a result they have thorough knowledge of every assignment under their control and are in a position to make amendments and take corrective action.

7. Quick Decision-Making:

Decentralisation brings decision making process closer to the scene of action. This leads to quicker decision-making of lower level since decisions do not have to be referred up through the hierarchy.

Disadvantages of Decentralisation:

Decentralisation can be extremely beneficial. But it can be dangerous unless it is carefully constructed and constantly monitored for the good of the company as a whole.

Some disadvantages of decentralisation are:

1. Uniform policies not Followed:

Under decentralisation, it is not possible* to follow uniform policies and standardised procedures. Each manager will work and frame policies according to his talent.

2. Problem of Co-Ordination:

Decentralisation of authority creates problems of co-ordination as authority lies dispersed widely throughout the organisation.

3. More Financial Burden:

Decentralisation requires the employment of trained personnel to accept authority, it involves more financial burden and a small enterprise cannot afford to appoint experts in various fields.

4. Require Qualified Personnel:

Decentralisation becomes useless when there are no qualified and competent personnel.

5. Conflict:

Decentralisation puts more pressure on divisional heads to realize profits at any cost. Often in meeting their new profit plans, bring conflicts among managers.

CHAPTER 3
INVENTORY CONTROL:

Definition and Meaning

According to Gordon Carson, "Inventory control is the process where by the investment in materials and parts carried in stocks is regulated, within pre-determined limits set in accordance with the inventory policy established by the management."

"Inventory control is a method where all stocks of goods are properly and promptly issued, accounted, and preserved in the best interest of an entity that handles its inventory."

Inventory control means to monitor the stock of goods used for production, distribution and captive (self) consumption.

For a specific time period, stock of goods are placed at some particular location. Stock of goods includes raw-materials, work in progress, finished goods, packaging, spares, components, consumable items, etc.

Inventory Control means maintaining the inventory at a desired level. The desired-level keeps on fluctuating as per the demand and supply of goods.

The concept or meaning of inventory control is depicted in the diagram.

keeps a record of inventory issued to the concerned department.	provides prompt and proper service to all concerned departments or units.	helps to maintain inventories at lowest costs.

helps to supply the inventory to different departments or units.	bifurcates high-value and low-value stock of goods.

focuses on location, storage, recording and accounting of inventories.	avoids over-stocking and under-stocking of raw-materials.

Inventory Control...

Following important points convey the broad meaning of inventory control:

Inventory Control mainly focuses on location, storage, recording the quantity, and accounting for the amount of inventories. It helps to supply inventories to different departments or units whenever demand requisition is raised. Mostly, it supplies inventories to the production department.

It keeps a record of inventory issued to the concerned department located at a specific place. It provides prompt and proper service to all concerned departments or units. It also helps to maintain inventories at lowest costs. It bifurcates high-value and low-value stock of goods. It also avoids over-stocking and under-stocking of raw-materials.

Types/Classification of Inventory:

The term inventory may be classified into two types namely:

1. Direct Inventories:

Direct inventories are those inventories that play a major role in the production and constitute a vital part of finished goods. These inventories can be easily assigned to specific physical units. Direct inventories may be categorised into four groups.

(i) Raw materials:

Raw materials are the physical resources to be used in the manufacture of finished products. They include materials that are in their natural or raw form. For example, cotton in the case of textile mill, sugarcane in the case of sugar factory, oil seeds in the case of an oil mill etc. The chief objective of keeping raw material is to ensure uninterrupted production in the event of delays in delivery and also to enjoy the economies of large scale buying.

(ii) Semi-finished Goods:

Semi-finished goods are those materials which are not cent per cent (100%) complete in all respects i.e., some processing still remains to be done before the product can be sold.

For example, a person who is engaged in the manufacture of furniture, may purchase unpolished furniture from market and sell it after polishing the same.

(iii) Finished Goods:

Finished goods are complete products that are ready for sale or distribution. For instance, in case of a hosiery factory, sweaters, shawls etc. are finished products.

(iv) Spare Parts:

Spare parts means duplicate parts of a machine. Usually, almost all the industrial concerns maintain spare parts of various machines which they use for manufacture. This will enable them to ensure smooth running of machines which in turn provide for uninterrupted production.

2. Indirect Inventories:

Indirect inventories include those items which are necessary for manufacturing but do not become component of the finished goods. They normally include petrol, maintenance materials, office materials, grease, oil lubricants etc. These inventories are used for ancillary purposes to the business and cannot be assigned to specific, physical units. These inventories may be used in the factory, the office or the selling and distribution divisions.

Some of the most important techniques of inventory control system are:

1. Setting up of various stock levels.
2. Preparations of inventory budgets.
3. Maintaining perpetual inventory system.
4. Establishing proper purchase procedures.

5. Inventory turnover ratios.

6. ABC analysis.

1. Setting up of various stock levels:

To avoid over-stocking and under stocking of materials, the management has to decide about the maximum level, minimum level, re-order level, danger level and average level of materials to be kept in the store.

These terms are explained below:

(a) Re-ordering level:

It is also known as 'ordering level' or 'ordering point' or 'ordering limit'. It is a point at which order for supply of material should be made.

This level is fixed somewhere between the maximum level and the minimum level in such a way that the quantity of materials represented by the difference between the re-ordering level and the minimum level will be sufficient to meet the demands of production till such time as the materials are replenished. Reorder level depends mainly on the maximum rate of consumption and order lead time. When this level is reached, the store keeper will initiate the purchase requisition.

Reordering level is calculated with the following formula:

Re-order level =Maximum Rate of consumption x maximum lead time

(b) Maximum Level:

Maximum level is the level above which stock should never reach. It is also known as 'maximum limit' or 'maximum stock'. The function of maximum level is essential to avoid unnecessary blocking up of capital in inventories, losses on account of deterioration and obsolescence of materials, extra overheads and temptation to thefts etc. This level can be determined with the following formula. Maximum Stock level = Reordering level + Reordering quantity - (Minimum Consumption x Minimum re-ordering period).

(c) Minimum Level:

It represents the lowest quantity of a particular material below which stock should not be allowed to fall. This level must be maintained at every time so that production is not held up due to shortage of any material.

It is that level of inventories of which a fresh order must be placed to replenish the stock. This level is usually determined through the following formula:

Minimum Level = Re-ordering level — (Normal rate of consumption x Normal delivery period)

(d) Average Stock Level:

Average stock level is determined by averaging the minimum and maximum level of stock.

The formula for determination of the level is as follows:

Average level =1/2 (Minimum stock level + Maximum stock level)

This may also be expressed by minimum level + 1/2 of Re-ordering Quantity.

(e) Danger Level:

Danger level is that level below which the stock should under no circumstances be allowed to fall. Danger level is slightly below the minimum level and therefore the purchases manager should make special efforts to acquire required materials and stores.

This level can be calculated with the help of following formula:

Danger Level =Average rate of consumption x Emergency supply time.

(f) Economic Order Quantity (E.O.Q.):

One of the most important problems faced by the purchasing department is how much to order at a time. Purchasing in large quantities involve lesser purchasing cost. But cost of carrying them tends to be higher. Likewise if purchases are made in smaller quantities, holding costs are lower while purchasing costs tend to be higher.

Hence, the most economic buying quantity or the optimum quantity should be determined by the purchase department by considering the factors such as cost of ordering, holding or carrying.

This can be calculated by the following formula:

$Q = \sqrt{2AS/I}$

where Q stands for quantity per order ;

A stands for annual requirements of an item in terms of rupees;

S stands for cost of placement of an order in rupees; and I stand for inventory carrying cost per unit per year in rupees.

2. Preparation of Inventory Budgets:

Organisations having huge material requirement normally prepare purchase budgets. The purchase budget should be prepared well in advance. The budget for production and consumable material and for capital and maintenance material should be separately prepared.

Sales budget generally provide the basis for preparation of production plans. Therefore, the first step in the preparation of a purchase budget is the establishment of sales budget. As per the production plan, material schedule is prepared depending upon the amount and return contained in the plan. To determine the net quantities to be procured, necessary adjustments for the stock already held is to be made. They are valued as standard rate or current market. In this way, material procurement budget is prepared.

The budget so prepared should be communicated to all departments concerned so that the actual purchase commitments can be regulated as per budgets.

At periodical intervals actuals are compared with the budgeted figures and reported to management which provide a suitable basis for controlling the purchase of materials.

3. Maintaining Perpetual Inventory System:

This is another technique to exercise control over

inventory. It is also known as automatic inventory system. The basic objective of this system is to make available details about the quantity and value of stock of each item at all times. Thus, this system provides a rigid control over stock of materials as physical stock can be regularly verified with the stock records kept in the stores and the cost office.

4. Establishing Proper Purchase Procedures:

A proper purchase procedure has to be established and adopted to ensure necessary inventory control. The following steps are involved.

(a) Purchase Requisition:

It is the requisition made by the various departmental heads or storekeeper for their various material requirements. The initiation of purchase begins with the receipts of a purchase requisition by the purchase department.

(b) Inviting Quotations:

The purchase department will invite quotations for supply of goods on the receipt of purchase requisition.

(c) Schedule of Quotations:

The schedule of quotations will be prepared by the purchase department on the basis of quotations received.

(d) Approving the supplier:

The schedule of quotations is put before the purchase committee who selects the supplier by considering factors like price, quality of materials, terms of payment, delivery schedule etc.

(e) Purchase Order:

It is the last step and the purchase order is prepared by the purchase department. It is a written authorisation to the supplier to supply a specified quality and quantity of material at the specified time and place mentioned at the stipulated terms.

5. Inventory Turnover Ratio:

These are calculated to minimise the inventory by the use of the following formula:

Inventory Turnover Ratio

= Cost of goods consumed/sold during the period/Average inventory held during the period

The ratio indicates how quickly the inventory is used for production. Higher the ratio, shorter will be the duration of inventory at the factory. It is the index of efficiency of material management.

The comparison of various inventory turnover ratios at different items with those of previous years may reveal the following four types of inventories:

(a) Slow moving Inventories:

These inventories have a very low turnover ratio. Management should take all possible steps to keep such inventories at the lowest levels.

(b) Dormant Inventories:

These inventories have no demand. The finance manager has to take a decision whether such inventories should be retained or scrapped based upon the current market price, conditions etc.

(c) Obsolete Inventories:

These inventories are no longer in demand due to their becoming out of demand. Such inventories should be immediately scrapped.

(d) Fast moving inventories:

These inventories are in hot demand. Proper and special care should be taken in respect of these inventories so that the manufacturing process does not suffer due to shortage of such inventories.

Perpetual inventory control system:

In a large b essential to have information about continuous availability of different types of materials and stores purchased, issued and their balance in hand. The perpetual inventory control system enables the manufacturer to know about the availability of these materials and stores without undergoing the cumbersome process of physical stock taking.

Under this method, proper information relating to receipt, issue and materials in hand is kept. The main objective of this system is to have accurate information about the stock level of every item at any time.

Perpetual inventory control system cannot-be successful unless and until it is accompanied by a system of continuous stock taking i.e., checking the total stock of the concern 3/4 times a year by picking 10/15 items daily (as against physical stock taking which takes place once a year).

The items are taken in rotation. In order to have more effective control, the process of continuous stock taking is usually undertaken by a person other than the storekeeper. This will check the functioning of storekeeper also. The items may be selected at random to have a surprise check. The success of the system of perpetual inventory control depends upon the proper implementation of the system of continuous stock taking.

6. ABC analysis:

In order to exercise effective control over materials, A.B.C. (Always Better Control) method is of immense use. Under this method materials are classified into three categories in accordance with their respective values.

Group 'A' constitutes costly items which may be only 10 to 20% of the total items but account for about 50% of the total value of the stores.

A greater degree of control is exercised to preserve these items. Group 'B' consists of items which constitutes 20 to 30% of the store items and represent about 30% of the total value of stores.

A reasonable degree of care may be taken in order to control these items. In the last category i.e. group 'Q' about 70 to 80% of the items is covered costing about 20% of the total value. This can be referred to as residuary category. A routine type of care may be taken in the case of third category.

This method is also known as 'stock control according to value method', 'selective value approach' and 'proportional parts value approach'.

If this method is applied with care, it ensures considerable reduction in the storage expenses and it is also greatly helpful in preserving costly items.

The A.B.C. Method of Inventory Control System: Advantages and Disadvantages!

In order to exercise effective control over materials, A.B.C. (Always Better Control) method is of immense use. Under this method materials are classified into three categories in accordance with their respective values. Group 'A' constitutes costly items which may be only 10 to 20% of the total items but account for about 50% of the total value of the stores.

A greater degree of control is exercised to preserve these items. Group 'B' consists of items which constitutes 20 to 30% of the store items and represent about 30% of the total value of stores.

A reasonable degree of care may be taken in order to control these items. In the last category i.e. group 'Q' about 70 to 80% of the items is covered costing about 20% of the total value. This can be referred to as residuary category. A routine type of care may be taken in the case of third category.

This method is also known as 'stock control according to value method', 'selective value approach' and 'proportional parts value approach'.

If this method is applied with care, it ensures considerable reduction in the storage expenses and it is also greatly helpful in preserving costly items.

Advantages of A.B.C. method of Inventory Control:

(i) It ensures control over the costly items in which a large amount of capital is invested.

(ii) It helps in developing scientific method of controlling inventories. Clerical costs are considerably reduced and stock is maintained at optimum level.

(iii) It helps in maintaining stock turnover rate at comparatively higher level through scientific control of inventories.

(iv) It ensures considerable reduction in the storage expenses. It results in stock carrying stock.

(v) It helps in maintaining enough safety stock for C category of items. The following graph demonstrates ABC inventory classification.

Disadvantages:

This analysis suffers from the following drawbacks:

1. This technique can be successfully employed only, if there is proper standardisation of materials in the store.

2. A good system of codification of materials should be in operation for the success of this analysis.

3. The analysis is based on monetary value of the items in use. Other important factors one ignored.

In spite of the above mentioned limitations, the ABC analysis is very popular method of inventory control. It is an effective instrument in reducing the cost of materials in the store house.

VED ANALYSIS :

The stores when subjected to analysis based on their criticality can be classified into vital, essential and desirable stores. This analysis is termed as VED analysis.

1. **Vital**: items without which treatment comes to standstill: i.e. non- availability can not be tolerated.

2. **Essential**: items whose non availability can be tolerated for 2-3 days, because similar or alternative items are available.

3. **Desirable:** items whose non availability can be tolerated for a long period. Although the proportion of vital, essential and desirable items varies from hospital to hospital depending on the type and quantity of workload, on an average vital items are 10%, essential items are 40% and desirable items make 50% of total items available.

Although not included in scientific VED analysis, in some public organizations which are static or inefficiently managed, there is a peculiar category of 'U' items which can be grouped as unnecessary. These unnecessary items get purchased due to the following reasons.

a)   Thoughtless continuation of previous purchase.

b)   Indifferent attitude towards hospital formulary.

c) Fear of change.

d) Poor supervision and control.

e) Unfair practice due to vested interest.

The vital items are stocked in abundance; essential items are stocked in medium amounts, and desirable items we stocked in small amounts.

By stocking the items in order of priority, vital and essential items are always in stock which means a minimum disruption in the services offered to the people.

Inventory is one of the major current assets to the organization. They are important input of final product. It is an area where significant cost savings can be made. Inventory decisions are high risk and high impact from the perspective of financial operation. Inventory, as current asset, differs from other current assets because only financial managers are not involved. Rather, all the functional areas, finance, marketing, production, and purchasing are involved.

The job of the financial manager is to reconcile the conflicting viewpoints of the various functional areas regarding the appropriate inventory levels in order to fulfill the overall objective of maximizing the owner"s wealth. Raw materials shortages can shutdown a manufacturing line or modify a production schedule, which, in turn introduces added expenses and potential for finished goods shortages. Just as shortages can disrupt planned marketing and manufacturing operations, over stocked inventories also create problems. Overstocks increases cost and reduce profitability through added warehousing, working capital requirements, deterioration, insurance, tax and obsolescence.

The importance of inventory control is listed in following points:

- Inventory control protects a company from fluctuations in demand of its products.
- It enables a company to provide better services to its customers.
- It keeps a smooth flow of raw-materials and aids in continuing production operations.
- It checks and maintains the right stock and reduces the risk of loss.
- It helps to minimise administrative workload, manpower requirement and even labour cost.
- It tries to protect fluctuation in output.
- It makes effective use of working capital by avoiding over-stocking.
- It helps to maintain a check on loss of materials due to carelessness or pilferage (stealing).
- It facilitates cost accounting activities.
- It avoids duplication in ordering of stock.

The following discussion briefly mentioned importance of inventory control.

1. Protects from fluctuations in demand

- Many a times, the demand forecast of a product is not accurate. There is always a small difference between the demand forecast and actual demand. However, sometimes, there is a big difference between the demand forecast and actual-demand.

- So, there are always chances of fluctuations in the demand of a material. These fluctuations can be adjusted if there are sufficient items in the stock of inventory.

2. Better services to customers

- If the company maintains a proper inventory of raw-materials, then it can complete its production in time. So, it can deliver the finished goods to the customers in time.

- Similarly, if the company has a proper inventory of finished goods, then it can satisfy the additional demand of the customers. So, inventory control helps the company to deliver goods at the right time as demanded by the customers.

- After making timely delivery, the company can concentrate on giving other services to the customers.

3. Continuity of production operations

- Proper inventory control helps to maintain continuity of production operations. This is because it maintains a smooth flow of raw materials. So, there are no shortages of raw-materials required for production process.

4. Reduces the risk of loss

- Proper inventory control helps to reduce the risk of loss due to obsolescence (outdated) or deterioration of items. This is because it checks all the items regularly.

- Furthermore, it sells all the slow-moving items, in time, at the market prices. It only maintains the right stock at all times. So, the chances of any item getting outdated is reduced.

5. Minimizes the administrative workload

- Proper inventory control helps to minimize the administrative work load of purchasing, inspection, warehousing, etc. This will reduce the manpower requirement and will minimize the labour cost too.

6. Protects fluctuation in output

- Inventory control tries to reduce the gap between planned production and actual production. There are cases where the production schedule cannot be followed because of:

- Sudden breakdown of machines,

- Problems in supply of materials,

- Sudden labour strikes,

- Loss due to failure of power supply, etc.

- In such cases, the difference between planned production and actual production can be bridged by inventories held in stock.

7. Effective use of working capital

- Proper inventory control helps to make effective use of working capital. Inventory control helps in maintaining the right amount of stocks of materials, components, etc. Over stocking is avoided. Therefore, the working capital will not be blocked in excess inventory.

8. Check on loss of materials

- Inventory control helps to maintain a check on the loss of materials due to carelessness or pilferage (stealing).

- If there is no proper inventory control, then there are more chances of carelessness and pilferage by the employees, especially in the store-keeping department.

9. Facilitates cost accounting activities

- Inventory control facilitates cost accounting activities. This is because, inventory control provides a means of allocating materials cost of products, departments or other operating accounts.

10. Avoids duplication in ordering

- Inventory control avoids duplication in ordering of stock. This is done by maintaining a separate purchase department. This department will do all the purchasing for the full organisation.

CHAPTER 4
DEVLOPING & LAUNCHING NEW PRODUCT & SERVICES

Process of developing a new product or service for the market.

This type of development is considered the preliminary step in product or service development and involves a number of steps that must be completed before the product can be introduced to the market. New product development may be done to develop an item to compete with a particular product/service or may be done to improve an already established product. New product development is essential to any business that must keep up with market trends and changes.

PROCESS OF NEW PRODUCT DEVELOPMENT

Every entrepreneur knows that productivity is one of the key ingredients for successful product development. One of the two key processes in Robert's Rules of Innovation is the NEW PRODUCT DEVELOPMENT PROCESS. A formalized, NPD process – also referred to and best practice: the Stage Gate Process – is a must, from simple to sophisticated.

The New Product Development process is often referred to as The Stage-Gate innovation process, developed by Dr. Robert G. Cooper as a result of comprehensive research on reasons why products succeed and why they fail.

When teams collaborate in developing new innovations, having the following eight ingredients mixed into your team's new product developmental repertoire will ensure that it's overall marketability will happen relatively quick, and accurately – making everyone productive across the board.

Step 1: Generating

Utilizing basic internal and external SWOT analyses, as well as current marketing trends, one can distance themselves from the competition by generating ideologies which take affordability, ROI, and widespread distribution costs into account. Lean, mean and scalable are the key points to keep in mind. During the NPD process, keep the system nimble and use flexible discretion over which activities are executed.

You may want to develop multiple versions of your road map scaled to suit different types and risk levels of projects.

Step 2: Screening The Idea

Wichita, possessing more aviation industry than most other states, is seeing many new innovations stop with Step 2 – screening. Do you go/no go? Set specific criteria for ideas that should be continued or dropped. Stick to the agreed upon criteria so poor projects can be sent back to the idea-hopper early on.

Because product development costs are being cut in areas like Wichita, "prescreening product ideas," means taking your Top 3 competitors' new innovations into account, how much market share they're chomping up, what benefits end consumers could expect etc.

An interesting industry fact: Aviation industrialists will often compare growth with metals markets; therefore, when Boeing is idle, never assume that all airplanes are grounded, per se.

Step 3: Testing The Concept

As Gaurav Akrani has said, "Concept testing is done after idea screening." And it is important to note, it is different from test marketing. Aside from patent research, design due diligence, and other legalities involved with new product development; knowing where the marketing messages will work best is often the biggest part of testing the concept. Does the consumer understand, need, or want the product or service?

Step 4: Business Analytics

During the New Product Development process, build a system of metrics to monitor progress. Include input metrics, such as average time in each stage, as well as output metrics that measure the value of launched products, percentage of new product sales and other figures that provide valuable feedback. It is important for an organization to be in agreement for these criteria and metrics.

Even if an idea doesn't turn into product, keep it in the hopper because it can prove to be a valuable asset for future products and a basis for learning and growth.

Step 5: Beta / Marketability Tests

Arranging private tests groups, launching beta versions, and then forming test panels after the product or products have been tested will provide you with valuable information allowing last minute improvements and tweaks. Not to mention helping to generate a small amount of buzz. WordPress is becoming synonymous with beta testing, and it's effective; Thousands of programmers contribute code, millions test it, and finally even more download the completed end-product.

Step 6: Technicalities + Product Development

Provided the technical aspects can be perfected without alterations to post-beta products, heading towards a smooth step 7 is imminent. According to Akrani, in this step, "The production department will make plans to produce the product. The marketing department will make plans to distribute the product. The finance department will provide the finance for introducing the new product".

As an example; In manufacturing, the process before sending technical specs to machinery involves printing MSDS sheets, a requirement for retaining an ISO 9001 certification (the organizational structure, procedures, processes and resources needed to implement quality management.)

In internet jargon, honing the technicalities after beta testing involves final database preparations, estimation of server resources, and planning automated logistics. Be sure to have your technicalities in line when moving forward.

Step 7: Commercialize

At this stage, your new product developments have gone mainstream, consumers are purchasing your good or service, and technical support is consistently monitoring progress. Keeping your distribution pipelines loaded with products is an integral part of this process too, as one prefers not to give physical (or perpetual) shelf space to competition.

Refreshing advertisements during this stage will keep your product's name firmly supplanted into the minds of those in the contemplation stages of purchase.

Step 8: Post Launch Review and Perfect Pricing

Review the NPD process efficiency and look for continues improvements. Most new products are introduced with introductory pricing, in which final prices are nailed down after consumers have 'gotten in'. In this final stage, you'll gauge overall value relevant to COGS (cost of goods sold), making sure internal costs aren't overshadowing new product profits.

You continuously differentiate consumer needs as your products age, forecast profits and improve delivery process whether physical, or digital, products are being perpetuated.

The entire new product development process is an ever evolving testing platform where errors will be made, designs will get trashed, and loss could be recorded. Having your entire team working in tight synchronicity will ensure the successful launch of goods or services, even if reinventing your own wheel. Productivity during product development can be achieved if, and only if, goals are clearly defined along the way and each process has contingencies clearly outlined on paper.

PROCESS OF ADOPTION OF NEW PRODUCT

The diffusion process describes the manner in which different members of the target market often accept and purchase a product. It spans the time from product introduction until market saturation:

1. Innovators are the first consumers to buy a new product. They are venturesome, willing to accept risk, socially aggressive, communicative, and cosmopolitan. It is necessary to determine which innovators are opinion leaders?those who influence others to purchase. This group represents 2.5 per cent of the target market.

2. Early adopters are the next consumers to buy a new product. They enjoy the leadership, prestige, and respect that early purchases bring. These consumers tend to be opinion leaders. They adopt new ideas but use discretion. This group represents 13.5 per cent of the market.

3. The early majority is the first part of the mass market to buy a product. They have status in their social class and are outgoing, communicative, and attentive to information cues. This group represents 34 per cent of the target market.

4. The late majority is the second part of the mass market to buy a product. They are less cosmopolitan and responsive to change. The late majority includes people with lower economic and social status, those past middle age, and skeptics. This group represents 34 per cent of the market.

5. Laggards are last to purchase. They are price conscious, suspicious of change, low in income and status, tradition bound, and conservative. Laggards do not adopt a product until it reaches maturity. Some firms ignore them because it can be difficult to market a product to this small group. However, a market segmenter may do well by concentrating on products for laggards.

CHARACTERISTICS OF NEW PRODUCT AFFECTING THE ADOPTION OF NEW PRODUCT :

➢ Relative advantage
➢ Compatibility
➢ Complexity
➢ Trialability
➢ Observability

Relative advantage is an observation of the advantages and benefits of adopting a specific innovation. An innovation is by definition an improvement over something already existing, so Rogers points out that the potential adopter must first calculate its relative strengths. What is the advantage of the iPad over a MacBook? What improvements does it hold? What other benefits in terms of mobility, ease-of-use, additional software packages, etc. does the innovation present? If someone finds an advantage in this new technology, the individual will be more likely to adopt it.

Another issue is **compatibility**. How well does the innovation fit into a person's needs, usage patterns and/or current value system? Adoption may have more to do with potential adopter than the characteristics of the innovation. An innovation that is more compatible with a person's lifestyle and cognitive characteristics is more likely to be assimilated into an individual's life.

A third characteristic is **complexity** and refers to the level of difficulty that the potential adopters encounter with the innovation. It is likely that the more complex or the more difficult an innovation is to understand, the less likely it will be adopted, and its diffusion will occur more slowly.

Observability completes our list of important characteristics identified by Rogers. An innovation will likely spread through the target population faster if the benefits are visible. "The Demo" by Douglas C. Engelbart was a 90-minute live demonstration of the interface technologies that highly influenced the trajectory of computer design that ultimately came out in the Apple Macintosh, including the first use of a mouse. The easier it is to see the advantages of an innovation, the faster it will diffuse throughout society.

CAUSES AND SUGGESTIONS OF PRODUCT FAILURE

1. Poor Market Research

Too many businesses dive into new markets, introduce new product lines or acquire new businesses without carrying out the necessary market research or due diligence.

The failure to conduct proper market analysis is a common oversight and as a result business owners and CEOs are often blindsided by their lack of preparedness in dealing with unanticipated events.

Solution:

To avoid this potentially ruinous scenario, companies should carry out a full-scale market analysis by setting up a web monitoring system that will surface any information relating to their target market: who are the main players? what is the price comparison and market performance of each competitor? In addition, companies should conduct customer sentiment analysis to discover reactions to competitor brands and to determine if there is sufficient demand for your product or service. Based on all of this data, you should have a clear idea of what level of market penetration can be achieved with your proposed new offering. The most important reason for carrying out a thorough market analysis is to avoid any major surprises which can derail your business early on.

2. Failure to Listen to Customers

Ignore your customers at your peril. It's a fairly basic piece of business advice and, one would think, an easy one to remember. But there are so many instances where customer needs are not given the priority they deserve, that it's still one of the number one reasons that businesses go to the wall each year. Getting a business off the ground takes a lot of focus and determination, along the way business owners and CEOs get distracted by other issues and customer needs start to slip down the list of priorities.

Solution:

One of the best ways to stay informed about your customer needs is to listen and learn about their purchasing habits, find out what trends they are following and get plugged in to the challenges they face in their daily lives. By tracking what your customers are saying about your company or brand on social media, web forums and discussion groups you have a clear idea about where to position your brand and how to anticipate evolving consumer trends.

3. Lack of Innovation

New technologies are emerging all the time and the companies who take advantage of the latest innovations are the ones who manage to stay ahead of the curve and achieve growth. Companies such as Kodak, Nokia and RIM have been severely penalized for neglecting to fight off the threat from breakthrough technologies and new innovations.

Solution:

By monitoring the latest technologies available in your market or scanning technology patents to see what's coming on stream in the future, your business will have more than a fighting chance of surviving the next wave of innovation.

Forward thinking business should set up an automated technology watch to provide answers to the following questions: What are the emerging technologies in our sector?

Which technologies used in other areas or sectors could benefit us by replacing our current technologies ?

Which technologies could be used to design new products, new packaging, new production or distribution methods?

Could any technologies be combined to improve our products?

How might emerging technologies affect our competitors or the arrival of new players?

Which companies master the key technologies we have identified and could we envisage an alliance or acquisition in the future?

4. Lack of Sales/Profit

Nowadays companies need to look beyond traditional sales channels to generate new customers. If your sales pipeline is running low you cannot possibly sustain your business into the future. Your growth potential is dependent on broadening and diversifying your customer base and that requires a steady stream of new sales prospects.

There is a wealth of information on the web which can be used to identify new sales opportunities. Once companies learn to harness this information correctly, the insight it will provide to front line sales teams will reap huge rewards.

Solution:

To immediately start growing the number of sales opportunities at their disposal, businesses should set up a 360 degree monitoring system which will notify sales teams of the following events:

– **New investments in plants/facilities:** this means the customer will be in a position to purchase new equipment.

– **New products launches:** this may lead to the setting up of new production lines.

– **New acquisitions:** will the customer modernize its acquisitions' existing machines/equipment?

– **New contracts:** Will there be a subsequent increase in production?

- **Personnel changes:** Should you get in touch with the new R&D director that has just been appointed?

PRODUCT MIX : MEANING AND COMPONENTS :

The term 'product mix' implies all the products offered by a firm for sale. It may consist of one line products or several allied product lines.

Product line refers to an assortment or class of similar or related products and services. They may be similar in technology, customers needs, channel used, market served or in some other respect. An individual product in a line is known as a product item. There are several product items in a product line. Product mix has three important aspects—width, depth and consistency. Width of the product mix is measured by the number and variety of product lines offered by a firm. It shows the degree of diversification of a firm's activities. The depth of product mix is determined by the number of items in a product line.

By offering several brands of a product, a firm can cater to widely varying needs and tastes of customers and thereby beat its competitors. For instance, the range of bathing soaps (Lifebouy, Lux, Rexona, Liril, etc.) offered by Hindustan Lever Ltd. shows the depth of its product line while the width of its product mix consists of Dalda Vanaspati, Close-up Toothpaste, Talcum powder, etc. in addition to the soaps.

The consistency of product mix refers to the degree of similarity between product lines in terms of their end-use, production requirements, price ranges, distribution channels, advertising media, etc.

These dimensions of the product mix serve as guides to decisions regarding the additions and deletions of product items and line. By increasing the consistency of product mix, a firm can reduce its costs of operations and acquire unparalleled reputation in the market.

Factors Affecting Product – Mix

1.   **Change in market demand:** the change in the demand of a product (due to change in habits, fashion, purchasing power, income, attitudes and preferences of consumers) affects the decision of product mix.

2.   **Cost of production:** if the company can develop a new product with the help of the same labour force, plant and machinery and techniques, it can decide to start the production of that product at lower cost.

3.   **Quantity of production:** if the production of new product is considered to be at a large scale and the company can add one more item to its product line just to get the economics of large scale production. Keeping in view its production capacity and other factors.

4.   **Advertising and distribution factors:** Advertising and distribution factors may be the one of the reason for the changes in production mix. If the advertising and distribution factors organization are the same, the company may take the decision to add one more item to its product line.

5.   **Use of residuals:** if residual can be used gainfully, the company can develop it's by products into the main products. For example, a sugar mill can profitably develop the production of paper card board or wine from biogases.

6.   **Change in company desire:** keeping in mind the objectives of the firm, maintaining or increasing the profitability of the concern, the firm may eliminate some of its unprofitable

processes or may start a new more profitable product. In this way, the firm tries to make its product mix an ideal one.

7. **Competitions actions and reactions:** the decision of adding or eliminating the product may be the reaction of competitor's actions. If company thinks that it can meet the competition well by making necessary changes in the size, colour, packing or price, it can make such changes.

8. **Change in purchasing power or behaviour of the customers:** if the numbers of customers are increased with the increase in their purchasing power or with the change in their buying habits, fashion, etc. the company may think of adding one or more product keeping mass production or increase in profitability in the mind.

9. **Full utilization of marketing capacity:** if the company is not getting desired results from the market, it can decide to stop the production of such a product and divert its resources to produce a new product or improve the existing product, according to the needs of the consumers.

10. **Financial resources:** finance is the life blood of the firm. Availability of the finance may necessarily some changes in the product of the company. If the company is short of finance or if the product is continuously going into loss the company may decide to drop such production similarly, if the company has sufficient funds, it may improve its products.

Product Repositioning:

Product Repositioning: Useful notes on Product Repositioning!

An effective positioning ties a company's product to a segment. The product is suitable for the customers of the target market but is singularly unsuitable for customers of other segments.

Unless there is lack of effective competition, a strongly positioned product would appeal only to a limited number of customers because it will have the benefits that the target market requires in an exaggerated form, while other benefits would hardly be provided.

So customers desiring benefits other than what the target market requires will not value the product. In an ideal situation, there would be a plethora of strongly positioned products, each serving a small set of customers.

Most companies want large number of customers for their products. To become attractive to a larger segment or multiple segments, the company provides an average level of all the benefits that the customers of the large segment or multiple segments desire from the product.

This average product is not particularly suitable for any set of customers, but it is also not very unsuitable for most of the customers.

In the absence of a product which will fit in with their requirements better, disparate sets of customers buy the product.

By diluting its positioning, the company has been able to sell to larger number of customers. But a more narrowly positioned company can come and attract sets of customers who find its product more suitable than the average product. More of such focused companies will come, eating into the market of the average product.

It is enticing to be able to serve a large or multiple segments with one product. But it turns into a dangerous strategy when other companies are willing to serve very small segments.

Repositioning:

Repositioning involves changing target markets or the differential advantage or both. There are four generic repositioning strategies.

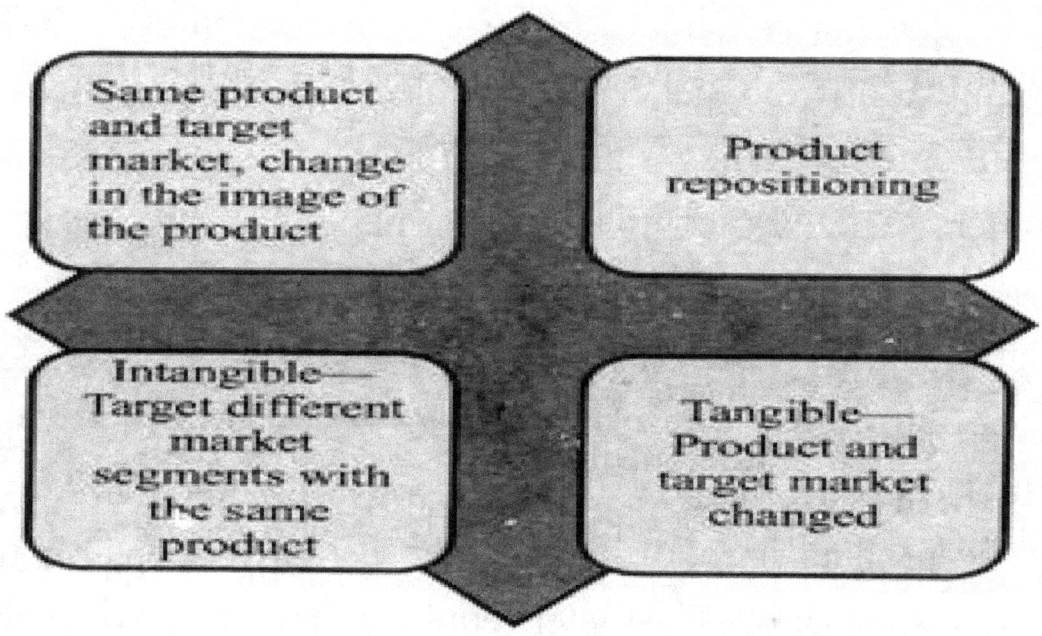

Repositioning

Same product and target market, change in the image of the product:

The product may be acceptable in functional terms but fails because it lacks the required image. The communication emanating from the company is overhauled.

The advertising message is changed. The contexts and the structure of the contexts in which the customers come into contact with the company are changed to reflect the new image.

It is not easy to effect such a repositioning. Because the company and its products do not change in any substantive way, it is very difficult for the company to believe that it is different from what it was earlier. And unless the company does not truly believe in its new image, it cannot communicate the new image effectively to its customers.

A company should engage in intensive internal communication to make its people feel differently about themselves before they start projecting the new image to the customers. Often a company may make superficial external changes, such as in packaging, to convey this type of repositioning to its internal and external customers. They do not work.

Product repositioning:

The product is modified to make it more acceptable to its present target market. Customer requirements may have changed and the product has to be modified to be able to serve the new needs effectively.

The company may have acquired new resources and competencies enabling it to modify the product so that it serves the target market better.

Intangible repositioning:

The company targets different market segments with the same product. The company is able to locate a segment which has requirements, similar to the requirements of the segments it is serving. The company retains its value proposition and offers it to new segments.

Tangible repositioning:

Both product and target market are changed. A company may decide to move up or down a market by introducing a new range of products to meet the needs of the new target customers.

Product diversification :

Growing sales of a new product in a new market.

Any modification of a current product that serves to expand the potential market implies that the company is following a strategy of product diversification.

The product diversification strategy is different from product development in that it involves creating a new customer base, which by definition expands the market potential of the original product. This is almost always done through brand extensions or new brands, but in some cases the product modification may "create" a new market by creating new uses for the product.

Teen People was an example of product diversification since it was a new product that expanded the market potential of the original product, People magazine. While some teenagers undoubtedly bought People magazine, they were not People's target market. Eventually, however, the product and Web site were merged into the People brand. Courtyard by Marriott and Fairfield Inn are other examples of product diversification since before Marriott offered those new brands they had little potential to expand sales in the business and budget categories. Marriott had business and budget guests, but they were not specifically targeted, so by concentrating on these two markets they were able to add to their market potential. It should be apparent why Marriott could not expand into such different categories with their original brand name.

When Heinz realized that children play with food and it would be more fun to play with ketchup if it were green or purple rather than red, they also were following a product diversification strategy since the market potential for ketchup increased from food to food plus play. Notice in this case that the brand name was unchanged.

Sometimes product diversification takes the form of a

product extension with the same brand name. Heinz's introduction of "black label" ketchup, Heinz Tomato Ketchup Blended with Balsamic Vinegar, targets the upscale buyer who might not consider Heinz's regular ketchup, thus expanding market potential.

The dangers of product diversification

The main dangers facing a company following a product diversification strategy for a brand are that it could fail to adequately understand the new customer base and that any new brand name may result in loss of meaning for the original brand and/or cannibalization of the original brand, particularly if it is a brand extension.

The risk of not understanding the new customer base is present as it is with market development.

References :

1. www.google.com
2. www.wikepedia.com

www.ingramcontent.com/pod-product-compliance
Lightning Source LLC
Chambersburg PA
CBHW080829180526
45168CB00006B/2623